**Strategic Studies Institute
and
U.S. Army War College Press**

THE GROWING COMPLEXITY OF SINO-INDIAN TIES

Harsh V. Pant

June 2014

*****

Comments pertaining to this report are invited and should be forwarded to: Director, Strategic Studies Institute and U.S. Army War College Press, U.S. Army War College, 47 Ashburn Drive, Carlisle, PA 17013-5010.

*****

This manuscript was funded by the U.S. Army War College External Research Associates Program. Information on this program is available on our website, *www.StrategicStudies Institute.army.mil*, at the Opportunities tab.

*****

*****

The Strategic Studies Institute and U.S. Army War College Press publishes a monthly email newsletter to update the national security community on the research of our analysts, recent and forthcoming publications, and upcoming conferences sponsored by the Institute. Each newsletter also provides a strategic commentary by one of our research analysts. If you are interested in receiving this newsletter, please subscribe on the SSI website at *www.StrategicStudiesInstitute.army.mil/newsletter*.

FOREWORD

With the world riveted by Chinese aggressiveness against Japan and Southeast Asian states in recent years, one country has not been particularly surprised: India. After all, New Delhi has been grappling with the challenge of China's rapid rise for some time now. An uneasiness exists between the two Asian giants, as they continue their ascent in the global interstate hierarchy. Even as they sign loftily worded documents year after year, the distrust between the two is actually growing at an alarming rate. True, economic cooperation and bilateral political as well as socio-cultural exchanges are at an all-time high; China is India's largest trading partner. Yet this cooperation has done little to assuage each country's concerns about the other's intentions. The two sides are locked in a classic security dilemma, where any action taken by one is immediately interpreted by the other as a threat to its interests.

India's challenge remains formidable. While it has not yet achieved the economic and political profile that China enjoys regionally and globally, India is increasingly bracketed with China as a rising or emerging power — or even a global superpower. Indian elites who have been obsessed with Pakistan for more than 60 years suddenly have found a new object of fascination. India's main security concern now is not the increasingly decrepit state of Pakistan but an ever more assertive China, a shift that is widely viewed inside India as one that should facilitate better strategic planning. India's defeat at Chinese hands in 1962 shaped the Indian elite's perceptions of China, and they are unlikely to alter them anytime soon. China is, thus, viewed by India as a growing, aggressive nationalistic power whose ambitions are likely to reshape the contours of the regional and global balance of power with deleterious consequences for Indian interests.

This monograph comes at a time when the Asian strategic landscape is undergoing a dramatic transformation. Accordingly, the author, Dr. Harsh V. Pant, examines the evolving trajectory of Indian policy towards China and underscores the implications for the region, and the United States in particular, at a time when U.S.-India ties are also evolving rapidly.

The Strategic Studies Institute is pleased to offer this monograph as part of its continuing effort to inform the debate on Asia's future, and to help strategic leaders to better understand the realities of the contemporary Asian strategic landscape.

DOUGLAS C. LOVELACE, JR.
Director
Strategic Studies Institute and
    U.S. Army War College Press

ABOUT THE AUTHOR

HARSH V. PANT is Professor of International Relations in the Defence Studies Department at King's College London, United Kingdom. He is also a Fellow (Non-Resident) with the Center for Strategic and International Studies, Washington, DC, and a Visiting Fellow with the Observer Research Foundation, New Delhi, India. He has been a Visiting Professor at the Indian Institute of Management, Bangalore; a Visiting Fellow at the Center for the Advanced Study of India, University of Pennsylvania; a Visiting Scholar at the Center for International Peace and Security Studies, McGill University, Montreal, Canada; and an Emerging Leaders Fellow at the Australia-India Institute, University of Melbourne, Australia. His current research is focused on Asian security issues. Dr. Pant's most recent books include *The US-India Nuclear Pact: Policy, Process and Great Power Politics* (Oxford University Press, 2011), *The Rise of China: Implications for India* (Cambridge University Press, 2012), and *The Rise of the Indian Navy: Internal Vulnerabilities, External Challenges* (Ashgate, 2012). Dr. Pant is a graduate of Delhi University, and holds an M.A. and an M.Phil. from Jawaharlal Nehru University and a Ph.D. in political science from the University of Notre Dame.

SUMMARY

According to most political observers, the global political architecture is undergoing a transformation with power increasingly shifting from the West to the East, in what has been called the Asian Century. The two most populous nations on the earth, China and India, are on their way to becoming economic power-houses and are shedding their reticence in asserting their global profiles, all of which makes their relation-ship of still greater importance for the international system. The future of this Asian Century will, to a large extent, depend upon the relationship between these two regional giants, and the bilateral relation-ship between them will define the contours of the new international political architecture in Asia and the world at large. This monograph examines the evolu-tion of Sino-Indian ties over the last few decades and the constraints that continue to inhibit this relation-ship from achieving its full potential before delineat-ing the implications of this for the United States and the wider international system.

THE GROWING COMPLEXITY
OF SINO-INDIAN TIES

INTRODUCTION

According to most political observers, the global political architecture is undergoing a transformation with power increasingly shifting from the West to the East, in what has been called the **Asian Century**. The two most populous nations on the earth, China and India, are on their way to becoming economic power-houses and are shedding their reticence in asserting their global profiles, all of which makes their relationship of still greater importance for the international system. The future of this Asian Century will, to a large extent, depend upon the relationship between these two regional giants, and the bilateral relationship between them will define the contours of the new international political architecture in Asia and the world at large. The importance of their relationship has not been lost on either country. In one of his meetings with the Indian Prime Minister, at the 2004 Asia-Europe Meeting (ASEM), former Chinese Premier Wen Jiabao is reported to have remarked that "when we shake hands, the whole world will be watching," a sentiment repeated by Indian Prime Minister Manmohan Singh during his visit to China in October 2013. As of today, however, the trajectory of the Sino-Indian relationship remains as complex as ever to decipher, despite some positive developments in the last few years. This monograph examines the evolution of Sino-India ties over the last few decades and the constraints that continue to inhibit this relationship from achieving its full potential before delineating the implications of this for the United States and the wider international system.

BACKGROUND

Initial Encounters.

As two ancient civilizations, India and China have had cultural and trade ties since at least the first century. The famous Silk Road allowed for economic and trade ties to develop between the two, with the transmission of Buddhism from India to China giving a further cultural dimension to the relationship between the two neighbors. The political ties between China and India, however, remained underdeveloped.

Independent India's first Prime Minister, Jawaharlal Nehru, saw anti-imperialist friendship between the two largest states of Asia as imperative if interference by the two external superpowers was to be avoided.[1] Solidarity with China was integral to Nehru's vision of Asian leadership. After the People's Republic of China (PRC) was established in 1949 and India established diplomatic ties with it in 1950, India not only advocated for the PRC's membership at the United Nations (UN) but also opposed attempts to condemn the PRC for its actions in Korea. Yet, the issue of Tibet soon emerged as the major bone of contention between China and India. China was suspicious of Indian designs on Tibet, which India sought to allay by supporting the *Seventeen-Point Agreement* between Tibetan delegates and China in 1951 that recognized PRC sovereignty over Tibet and guaranteed the existing socio-political arrangements of Tibet. India and China signed the famed *Panchshila* agreement in 1954 that underlined the *Five Principles of Peaceful Coexistence* as forming the basis of their bilateral relationship.[2] These principles included mutual respect for each other's territorial integrity and sovereignty; mutual nonaggression; mu-

2

tual noninterference in each other's internal affairs; equality and mutual benefit; and peaceful coexistence. These were the hey-days of Sino-Indian ties, with the *Hindi-China bhai-bhai* ("Indians and Chinese are brothers") phrase a favorite slogan for the seeming camaraderie between the two states.

But that was not to last long. Soon the border dispute between China and India escalated and led to the 1962 Sino-Indian war.[3] Though a short war, it was to have a long-lasting impact on Sino-Indian ties. It demolished Nehru's claims of Asian solidarity, and the defeat at the hands of the Chinese psychologically scarred Indian military and political elites. It led to China developing close ties with India's neighboring adversary, Pakistan, resulting in what is now widely considered an "all-weather" friendship. China supported Pakistan in its 1965 and 1971 wars with India and helped in the development of its nuclear weapons arsenal. Meanwhile, the Indian nuclear weapons program was accelerated in light of China's testing of nuclear weapons in 1964.

The border issue remains a major obstacle in Sino-Indian ties, with minor skirmishes at the border continuing since 1962. As China and the United States became closer after their rapprochement in 1972, India gravitated to the former Soviet Union to balance the China-U.S.-Pakistan axis. It was in 1988 that then Indian Prime Minister Rajiv Gandhi turned a new leaf in Sino-Indian ties when he went to Beijing and signed an agreement that aimed at achieving a "fair and reasonable settlement while seeking a mutually acceptable solution to the border dispute."[4] The visit saw a Joint Working Group (JWG) set up to explore the boundary issue and examine probable solutions to the problem.

However, bilateral relations between India and the PRC touched their nadir in the immediate aftermath of India's nuclear tests in May 1998. China had been singled out as the "number one" security threat for India by India's Defence Minister just before the nuclear tests.[5] After the tests, the Indian Prime Minister wrote to the U.S. President justifying Indian nuclear tests as a response to the threat posed by China:

> We have an overt nuclear weapons state [China] on our borders, a state which committed armed aggression against India in 1962. Although our relations with that country have improved in the last decade or so, an atmosphere of distrust persists mainly due to the unresolved border problem. To add to the distrust, that country has materially helped another neighbour of ours [Pakistan] to become a covert nuclear weapons state.[6]

Not surprisingly, China reacted strongly, with diplomatic relations between the two countries plummeting to an all time low.

However, after more than a decade, the relations between the two countries, at least superficially, seem to be on a much firmer footing as they have tried to reduce the prospect for rivalry and expand areas of cooperation. The visit of the Indian External Affairs Minister to China in 1999 marked the resumption of high-level dialogue, as the two sides declared that they were not threats to each other. A bilateral security dialogue was also initiated that has helped the two countries in openly expressing and sharing their security concerns with each other. Both China and India continue to emphasize that neither side should let differences act as an impediment to the growth of functional cooperation elsewhere between the two states. India and China also decided to expedite the process of demarcation of the Line of Actual Control (LAC), and the JWG on the boundary question, set up in 1988, has been meeting regularly. As a first step in this direction, the two countries exchanged border maps on the least controversial Middle Sector of the LAC. More recently, both nations agreed on *Political Parameters and Guiding Principles for the Settlement of the India-China Boundary Question* (2005), broad principles to govern the parameters of any dispute settlement. China has expressed its desire to seek a fair resolution to the vexed boundary issue on the basis of "mutual accommodation, respect for history, and accommodation of reality."[7]

Diplomacy of Declarations.

Former Indian Prime Minster Atal Bihari Vajpayee visited China in June 2003, the first by an Indian Premier in a decade. The *Joint Declaration* signed during this visit expressed the view that China was not a threat to India.[8] The two states appointed Special Representatives in order to impart momentum to border negotiations that have lasted now for more than 20 years, with the Prime Minister's principal secretary becoming India's political-level negotiator, replacing the India-China JWG. India and China also decided to hold their first joint naval and air exercises. More significantly, India acknowledged China's sovereignty over Tibet and pledged not to allow anti-China political activities in India. For its part, China seems to have finally acknowledged India's 1975 incorporation of the former monarchy of Sikkim, by agreeing to open a trading post along the border with the former kingdom and later by rectifying its official maps to include

5

Sikkim as part of India.[9] After being closed for 60 years, the Nathu La pass, a traditional trading post between Tibet and Sikkim, was reopened in 2006. High-level political interactions have continued unabated since then. The two states have set up institutionalized defense consultation mechanisms to reduce suspicions and identify areas of cooperation on security issues.

Soon after assuming office, the Manmohan Singh government made it clear that it desired closer ties with China and would continue to work towards improving bilateral relations with China. India's former national security advisor, J. N. Dixit, wrote that "the Congress will continue the process of normalizing, strengthening and expanding India's relations with China, which is the most important factor affecting Asian security and stability."[10] In his first address to the nation, Prime Minister Singh also emphasized the carrying forward of the process of further development and diversification of Sino-Indian relations.[11]

When Singh visited China in 2008, the two states signed *A Shared Vision for the 21st Century of the People's Republic of China and the Republic of India* declaration: "to promote the building of a harmonious world of durable peace and common prosperity through developing the Strategic and Cooperative Partnership for Peace and Prosperity between the two countries."[12] Support for the earlier *Agreement on Political Parameters and Guiding Principles for the Settlement of the China-India Boundary Question* (2005) was reiterated. The two sides have decided to elevate the boundary negotiations to the level of a strategic dialogue, with plans for a hotline between the Indian Prime Minister and the Chinese Premier as a means to remove misunderstanding and reduce tensions at the earliest possible instance. Their public vision suggested that this relationship would have "a positive influence on the future of the international system."[13] The two nations signed the Border Defence Cooperation Agreement (BDCA) in 2013 aimed at curbing incidents along the border that inflame public passions.

This has been ongoing at a time when economic relations between the two have been burgeoning, with China emerging as India's largest trading partner. The Sino-Indian trade is on course to achieve a volume of $100 billion by 2015, providing a basis for long-term engagement.

Global Engagement.

It is at the international level, however, that India and China have found some real convergence of interests. Both share similar concerns about U.S. international dominance, the threat of fundamentalist religious and ethnic movements in the form of terrorism, and the need to accord primacy to economic development. India and China have both expressed concern about the U.S. use of military power around the world, and both were publicly opposed to the war in Iraq. This was merely a continuation of the desire of both states to oppose the U.S. hyperpuissance since the end of the Cold War.

Both China and India, much like other major powers in the international system, favor a multipolar world order where U.S. unipolarity remains constrained by the other "poles" in the system. China and India zealously guard their national sovereignty and have been wary of U.S. attempts to interfere in what they see as domestic affairs of other states, be it in Serbia, Kosovo, Iraq, or more recently, Libya and Syria. Both took strong exception to the U.S. air strikes on Iraq in 1998, the U.S.-led air campaign against Yugoslavia in 1999, and the U.S. campaign against Saddam Hussein, arguing that these violated the sovereignty of both countries and undermined the authority of the UN system.[14] China and India share an interest in resisting interventionist foreign policy doctrines emanating from the West, particularly the United States, and display "conservative attitudes on the prerogatives of sovereignty."[15]

China and India have coordinated their efforts on issues as wide-ranging as climate change, trade negotiations, energy security, and the global financial crisis. Both nations favor more democratic international economic regimes. Sino-Indian coordination on climate change, global trade negotiations, as well as in demanding a restructuring of financial institutions in view of the world economy's shifting center of gravity has had a significant impact on the course of international politics over the last few years. It is being argued that the forces of globalization have led to a certain convergence of Sino-Indian interests in the economic realm, as the two nations become even more deeply engaged in the international trading economy and more integrated in global financial networks.[16] The two have strongly resisted efforts by the United States and other developed nations to link global trade to labor and environmental standards, realizing clearly that this would put them at a huge disadvantage in relation to the developed world, thereby hampering their drive towards economic development, the number one priority for both countries. Both have committed themselves to crafting joint Sino-Indian positions in the World Trade Organization (WTO) and global trade negotiations in the hope that this might provide them greater negotiating leverage over other developed states. They would like to see further liberalization of agricultural trade in the developed countries, tightening of the rules on anti-dumping measures, and ensuring that nontrade related issues such as labor and environment are not allowed to come to the WTO. Both have fought carbon emission caps proposed by the industrialized world and have resisted Western pressure to open their agricultural markets.

It is against an increasingly complex strategic background that states such as China and India are trying to shape their own energy policies. Their approach toward their energy predicament remains rather traditional insofar as it is largely state-centric, supply-side biased, mainly reliant on oil, and tends to privilege self-sufficiency.[17] It is toward an aggressive pursuit of energy resources, particularly oil, across the globe that China and India seem to have focused their diplomatic energies in recent years, with some far-reaching implications.

Both China and India are feeling the pressure of diminishing oil discoveries and flat-lined oil production at a time when expansion of their domestic economies is rapidly increasing demand for energy. They have made energy the focal point of their diplomatic overtures to states far and wide. More significantly, faced with a market in which politics has an equal, if not greater, influence on price as does economics, the two have also decided to coordinate their efforts to secure energy resources overseas. In essence, China and India plan to work together to secure energy resources without unnecessarily bidding up the price of those resources, thereby agreeing to a consumer's cartel representing 2.3 billion potential consumers. Together, their combined markets and purchasing power offers an extremely attractive partner to energy-producing states, especially the ones that face Western pressure over their human rights records or the nature of their political institutions.

It has been argued by many that cooperation between China and India on energy issues is the only way ahead if both states want to gain economies of scale and negotiation muscle. In many ways, both states face similar constraints in achieving energy security and a coordinated approach would benefit them both. Competition only ends up driving up the costs of acquisition, thereby diminishing future returns. There has been a recognition of this at the highest levels of the government in both states.

China and India have signed a range of memoranda on energy cooperation that covers a full scope of areas, including upstream exploration and production, the refining and marketing of petroleum products and petrochemicals, the laying of national and transnational oil and gas pipelines, frontier and cutting-edge research and development, and the promotion of environment-friendly fuels.[18]

The two states have agreed to strengthen the exchange of information when bidding for oil resources in a third party country in order to realize mutual benefit. China has pledged to promote cooperation with India in civil nuclear energy and to view this cooperation in the context of climate change and increasing nonpolluting sources in the energy mix. The former Indian petroleum minister, Mani Shankar Aiyar, made it clear that he thought that India and China joining hands to bid jointly for oil and gas assets under a "monopsonistic" arrangement was much better than the two states competing in their quest for energy resources.[19] He had even floated the idea of an Asian energy grid that might follow the trajectory of the European Coal and Steel Community, which grew into the European Union (EU). According to Aiyar, "India and China don't have to go through fratricide in order to arrive at the conclusion that it is better to cooperate on energy security."[20]

From Global to Bilateral: Without Much Success.

The attempt on the part of China in recent years has been to build its bilateral relationship with India on the basis of the larger worldview of international politics on the part of both nations. As New Delhi and Beijing discovered a distinct convergence of their interests on the world stage, they have used it to strengthen their bilateral relations. They have established and maintained regular reciprocal high-level visits between political leaders. There has been a serious attempt to improve trade relations and China has sought to compartmentalize intractable issues with India that make it difficult for their bilateral relationship to move forward.

At the global level, the rhetoric is all about cooperation, and indeed the two sides have worked together on climate change, global trade negotiations and demanding a restructuring of global financial institutions in view of the global economy's shifting center of gravity.[21] At the bilateral level, however, mounting tensions reached an impasse in 2009, when China took its territorial dispute with India all the way to the Asian Development Bank. There China blocked India's application for a loan that included money for development projects in the Indian state of Arunachal Pradesh, which China continues to claim as part of its own territory.[22] The suggestion by the Chinese to the U.S. Pacific Fleet commander in 2009 that the Indian Ocean should be recognized as a Chinese sphere of influence also raised hackles in New Delhi.[23] China's lack of support for the U.S.-India civilian nuclear energy cooperation pact, which it tried to block at the Nuclear Suppliers Group (NSG), and its obstructionist stance about bringing the terror masterminds of the November 2008 Mumbai attacks to justice have further strained ties.

Sino-Indian frictions are growing, and the potential for conflict remains high. Alarm is rising in India because of frequent and strident Chinese claims about the Line of Actual Control in Arunachal Pradesh and Sikkim, where Indians have complained of a dramatic rise in Chinese intrusions into Indian territory over the last few years, most along the border in Arunachal Pradesh, which China refers to as "Southern Tibet." China has upped the ante on the border issue. It has been regularly protesting against the Indian Prime Minister's visits to Arunachal Pradesh over the last few years, asserting its claims over the territory. What has caught most observers of Sino-Indian ties by surprise, however, is the vehemence with which Beijing has contested recent Indian administrative and political action in the state, even denying visas to Indian citizens of Arunachal Pradesh. The recent rounds of boundary negotiations have been a disappointing failure, with a growing perception in India that China is less willing to adhere to earlier political understandings about how to address the boundary dispute.

The possibility of an intimate U.S.-India military relationship has generated fears of encirclement in Beijing. India's position astride China's key maritime shipping lanes has made the prospect of a Washington-Delhi axis particularly worrisome. Pakistan, of course, has always been a crucial foreign policy asset for China, but with India's rise and U.S.-India rapprochement, its role in China's grand strategy is bound to grow even further. Not surprisingly, recent revelations about China shifting away from a 3-decades' old cautious approach on Jammu and Kashmir, increasing its military presence in Pakistan, planning infrastructure linking Xinjiang and Gwadar, issuing stapled visas to residents of Jammu and Kashmir and supplying nuclear reactors to Pakistan, all confirm a new intensity behind China's old strategy of using Pakistan to secure its interests in the region. China has gone even further than Pakistan in defining the Kashmir issue. While Pakistan insists that Kashmir is a disputed territory, recent Chinese positions have made it clear that Beijing believes Pakistan occupied Kashmir (PoK) is Pakistani territory with India's Kashmir state being the only part of the province that is disputed.[24] Pakistan seems to have ceded responsibility for the Gilgit-Baltistan area of PoK to China as the reported presence of 7,000-10,000 People's Liberation Army (PLA) troops there underscores.[25] The real concern for India, however, is the number of projects that China has undertaken in these areas, and that footprint is likely to increase.[26]

China's economic transformation has given it the capability to emerge as a major military power as it continues to announce double-digit increases in its military spending. China's military may or may not be able to take on the United States in the next few years, but it will surely become the most dominant force in Asia. As a consequence of its growing capabilities, China has started asserting its military profile more significantly than before. Since 2009, Chinese vessels have been tackling Somali pirates in the Middle East, the first time Chinese vessels operated outside Asia. Beijing has also started sending combat troops abroad in support of UN peacekeeping efforts.

China's sustained military build-up will continue over the next few years and will pose a challenge to Indian military planners as the Indian military's modernization program is fast losing momentum. As the policy paralysis post-Mumbai has revealed, India seems to have lost even its conventional superiority over Pakistan. The real challenge for India, however, lies in China's rise as a military power. India is speeding up its defense procurement but the process remains mired in bureaucratese and lacks any sense of strategic direction.[27] According to an estimate by the Indian government's own China Study Group, China now possesses the capability to move more than 10,000 troops to the Indian border in 20 to 25 days, compared to 3 to 6 months a decade ago.[28] This is possible because of China's efficient border management, and it has forced India into urgently constructing border roads. By engaging in repeated, though controlled, provocations, the Chinese military is carefully probing how far it can push India. The new military restiveness on the Sino-Indian border does not bode well for India as the military balance along the long and contested border is rapidly altering in Beijing's favor. It is not without reason that China has upgraded its military and civilian infrastructure in Xinjiang and Tibet. As a consequence, Tibet has become a militarized zone.

CURRENT ISSUES

China's Naval Power Projection.

China is acquiring naval bases along the crucial choke points in the Indian Ocean not only to serve its economic interests but also to enhance its strategic presence in the region. There is enough evidence to suggest that China is comprehensively building up its maritime power in all dimensions.[29] It is China's growing dependence on maritime space and resources that is reflected in the Chinese aspiration to expand its influence and ultimately to dominate the strategic environment of the Indian Ocean region. Its growing reliance on bases across the Indian Ocean region is a response to its perceived vulnerability, given the logistical constraints that it faces due to the distance of the Indian Ocean waters from its own area of operation. Yet, China is consolidating power over the South China Sea and the Indian Ocean with an eye on India, something that comes out clearly in a secret memorandum issued by the Director of the General Logistic Department of the PLA: "We can no longer accept the Indian Ocean as only an ocean of the Indians. . . . We are taking armed conflicts in the region into account."[30]

China has deployed its *Jin* class submarines at a base near Sanya on the southern tip of Hainan Island in the South China Sea, raising alarm in India as the base is merely 1,200 nautical miles from the Malacca Strait and will be its closest access point to the Indian Ocean. The base also has an underground facility that can hide the movement of submarines, making them difficult to detect.[31] The concentration of strategic naval forces at Sanya will further propel China towards a consolidation of its control over the surrounding Indian Ocean region. The presence of access tunnels on the mouth of the deep water base is particularly troubling for India as it will have strategic implications in the Indian Ocean region, allowing China to interdict shipping at the three crucial choke points in the Indian Ocean. The choice of Hainan is poor, but no alternatives exist as other places are hemmed in by islands. So China's chief maritime nuclear base is also what is for now her southernmost point. She would want the waters around it clear so that, among other things, no one can track her submarines.

As the ability of China's navy to project power in the Indian Ocean grows, India is likely to feel even more vulnerable despite enjoying distinct geographical advantages in the region. China's growing naval presence in and around the Indian Ocean region is troubling for India as it restricts India's freedom to maneuver in the region. Of particular note is what has been termed China's "string of pearls" strategy that has significantly expanded its strategic depth in India's backyard.[32]

This string of pearls strategy of bases and diplomatic ties include the Gwadar port in Pakistan, naval bases in Burma, electronic intelligence gathering facilities on islands in the Bay of Bengal, funding construction of a canal across the Kra Isthmus in Thailand, a military agreement with Cambodia, and building up of forces in the South China Sea.[33] Some of the Indian claims relating to these developments are exaggerated as has been the case with the Chinese naval presence in Burma. The Indian government, for example, had to concede in 2005 that reports of China turning the Coco Islands in Burma into a naval base were incorrect, and that there were, indeed, no naval bases in Burma.[34] Yet the Chinese thrust into the Indian Ocean is gradually becoming more pronounced. The Chinese may not have a naval base in Burma but they are involved in the upgrade of infrastructure in the Coco Islands and may be providing some limited technical assistance to Burma. Given that almost 80 percent of China's oil passes through the Strait of Malacca, it is reluctant to rely on U.S. naval power for unhindered access to energy and so has decided to build up its naval power at "choke points" along the sea routes from the Persian Gulf to the South China Sea. China is also courting other states in South Asia by building container ports in Bangladesh at Chittagong and in Sri Lanka at Hambantota. Consolidating its access to the Indian Ocean, China has signed an agreement with Sri Lanka to finance the development of the Hamban-tota Development Zone, which includes a container port, a bunker system, and an oil refinery. It is pos-sible that the construction of these ports and facilities around India's periphery by China can be explained away on purely economic and commercial grounds but for India this looks like a policy of containment by other means.

China's involvement in the construction of the deep-sea port of Gwadar has attracted a lot of atten-tion due to its strategic location, about 70 kilometers from the Iranian border and 400 kilometers east of the Strait of Hormuz, a major oil supply route. It has been suggested that it will provide China with a listening post from where it can "monitor US naval activity in the Persian Gulf, Indian activity in the Arabian Sea, and future US-Indian maritime cooperation in the In-dian Ocean."[35] Though Pakistan's naval capabilities do not, on their own, pose any challenge to India, the combinations of Chinese and Pakistani naval forces can, indeed, be formidable for India to counter.

China would certainly like to play a greater role in the region, protect and advance its interests, espe-cially its commerce, as well as countering India. But given the immense geographical advantages that In-dia enjoys in the Indian Ocean, China will have great difficulty in exerting as much sway there as India can. China's assertion of its naval prowess, however, is raising vexing issues regarding the role of Indian naval power in the Indian Ocean. The Indian and Chinese navies are growing and acquiring the capability to operate at long distances. The Sino-Indian strategic relationship is rapidly evolving and tensions are building up as was underlined in an incident in 2009 when an Indian *Kilo* class submarine and Chinese warships, on their way to the Gulf of Aden to patrol the pirate-infested waters, reportedly engaged in rounds of maneuvering as they tried to test for weaknesses in each other's sonar systems. The Chinese media reported that its warships forced the Indian submarine to the surface, which was strongly denied by the Indian navy.[36] Another incident led to an unidentified Chinese warship demanding that the INS *Airavat,* an Indian amphibious assault vessel, identify itself and explain its presence in the South China Sea after the vessel left Vietnamese waters in July 2011.[37] The Indian warship was completing a scheduled port call in Vietnam and was in international waters. Though the Indian Navy promptly denied that a Chinese warship had confronted its assault vessel, it did not completely deny the factual basis of the report. Maritime friction is likely to grow as the Indian Navy tries to expand its footprint in the South China Sea and the Western Pacific even as the Chinese Navy increases its presence in the Indian Ocean. It is India's fears and perceptions of the growing naval prowess of China in the Indian Ocean that is driving Indian naval posture.

The Nuclear Issue.

China remains the only major power in the world that refuses to discuss nuclear issues with India for fear that this might imply a de facto recognition of India's status as a nuclear power. It continues to insist on the sanctity of UN Resolution 1172, which calls for India (and Pakistan) to give up its nuclear weapons program and join the Nuclear Non-Proliferation Treaty (NPT) as a non-nuclear weapons state.[38] For the same reason, China refuses to discuss nuclear confidence building and risk reduction measures with India. It is interesting that a large section of China's political and military elite views India's nuclear tests in 1998, not as an attempt by India to address its security concerns, but rather a U.S. attempt to contain China insofar as the United States "allowed" India to go nuclear.[39]

The U.S.-India civilian nuclear energy cooperation pact came as a shock to Beijing. China made every possible effort to scuttle the deal until the last minute. It made its displeasure with the nuclear pact clear by asking India to sign the NPT and dismantle its nuclear weapons. Since the U.S.-India deal is in many ways a recognition of India's rising global profile, China, not surprisingly, was not very happy with the outcome and quickly declared that it would be selling new nuclear reactors to Pakistan. It was a not so subtle message to the United States that if Washington decided to play favorites, China also retained the same right.

Beijing viewed the nuclear deal through the lens of the global balance of power and was perturbed about the U.S. desire to build India as a balancer in the region. China was opposed to an exemption for India from the NSG guidelines, even threatening to walk out of the NSG proceedings at Vienna in 2008 in its attempts to derail negotiations at the 11th hour. The Chinese leadership refused to receive the Indian Prime Minister's call during the crisis. Only when the other states were persuaded by the United States to support the deal and China realized that it would be the last state standing, did it back off from its obstructionist stance. China's actions with regard to the nuclear pact have conveyed to India that even as India tries hard to break out of the straitjacket of being a South Asian power by forging a strategic partnership with the United States, China will do its utmost to contain India by building up its neighboring adversaries.

To counter the U.S.-India nuclear pact, China has decided to allow its state entities to supply two new nuclear reactors to Pakistan. Chinese authorities have confirmed that the state-owned China National Nuclear Corporation has signed an agreement with Pakistan for two new nuclear reactors at the Chashma site—Chashma III and Chashma IV—in addition to the two it is already working on in Pakistan. This action of China will be in clear violation of the NSG guidelines that forbid nuclear transfers to countries not signatories to the NPT or which adhere to comprehensive international safeguards on their nuclear program. China has suggested that "there are compelling political reasons concerning the stability of South Asia to justify the exports," echoing Pakistan's oft-repeated complaint that the U.S.-India nuclear pact has upset stability in the region by assisting India's strategic program.[40] Unlike the much debated U.S.-India nuclear pact, the Sino-Pakistani agreement is mired in secrecy with Beijing even ready to short-circuit the NSG process. Disregarding Indian and global concerns, China has contended that the sale of two new reactors is "grandfathered" from before it joined the NSG in 2004, and therefore an exemption from the NSG is not required. The decision to supply reactors to Pakistan, a nonsignatory to the NPT and with a record of dealing with North Korea, Iran, and Libya, reflects China's growing diplomatic confidence and underscores its view of Pakistan as a prized South Asian strategic power.

The Pakistani nuclear weapons program is essentially an extension of the Chinese one. China's crucial role in the development of Pakistan's nuclear infrastructure is well documented. Although China has long denied helping any nation attain a nuclear capability, the father of Pakistan's nuclear weapons program, Abdul Qadeer Khan, himself has acknowledged the crucial role China has played in his nation's nuclear weaponization by gifting 50 kilograms of weapons grade enriched uranium, drawings of the nuclear weapons, and tons of uranium hexafluoride for Pakistan's centrifuges. This is perhaps the only case where a nuclear weapons state has actually passed on weapons grade fissile material as well as a bomb design to a non-nuclear weapons state. The Sino-Pakistani collusion on nuclear issues has continued despite China being a signatory to the NPT.

Moreover, while both India and China have a "no-first-use" nuclear doctrine, China's doctrine is not applicable to India as India is not a party to the NPT. China's "minimum nuclear doctrine" has changed to "limited nuclear doctrine," suggesting a nuclear warfighting capability. It has been estimated that the Chinese nuclear arsenal of about 500 warheads comprises 200 strategic warheads, while the rest are of a tactical nature. Those tactical warheads are deployed at about 20 locations in China, including Tibet, and are well integrated at the operational level. On the other hand, India's no-first-use pledge and minimum deterrence posture have precluded the possession of tactical nuclear weapons, leading to a serious operational shortcoming as well as depriving India of an appropriate level of deterrence against China. India may well have to attain parity with China's strategic nuclear forces in order to successfully counter its aggressively coercive bargaining vis-à-vis India.

Among the five nuclear powers, it is China that is making the most dramatic advances in its nuclear force with the introduction and deployment of new generation land-based ballistic missiles and nuclear submarines. Sino-Indian competition in the nuclear arena is intensifying after China decided to upgrade its missile facilities near Tibet in 2007, bringing targets in northern India within range of its forces. The Indian Army is in the process of incorporating Agni-III, its intermediate range missile, which is capable of reaching all of China's major cities, and has successfully tested the nuclear-capable, 5,000-kilometer range Agni-V ballistic missile to bolster its deterrence posture against China. India's no-first-use nuclear doctrine relies fundamentally on a credible second strike capability. The Agni-V, by bringing the Chinese heartland into India's missile orbit, makes the Sino-Indian nuclear dynamic more stable than before.

India has also shifted a squadron of its most advanced multirole fighter aircraft, Su-30MKI, to a base just 150 kilometers from the disputed Sino-Indian border. New Delhi is considering missile defense systems, including the U.S. Patriot-3 and Israel's Iron Dome and David's Sling, in response to the Chinese military's plan to place Dongfeng-21 medium-range ballistic missiles on the Tibetan plateau.[41] India's indigenous ballistic missile defense (BMD) program has been accelerated and is now considered ready for integration into the nation's air defense assets. Its Defence Research and Development Organisation (DRDO) has suggested that by 2013–14, the system would include phase-I missiles, capable of neutralizing incoming missiles at the 2,000-kilometer range. With an eye on China, phase-II will be aimed at thwarting threats from missiles up to 5,000 kilometers.[42] After China demonstrated its test-firing capability in space, India has suggested that it remains open to extending the BMD program to that arena, although its official policy remains one of staunch opposition to any attempt to place weapons in space.

Border Tensions.

China has vigorously asserted its old claims along the border with India and has combined the assertion with aggressive patrolling. Violating the 1993 India-China agreement on peace and tranquility on the Line of Actual Control, Chinese troops have been engaging Indian troops in verbal abuses, asking them to leave their own territory. Even as India considered the Sikkim border issue settled, repeated Chinese incursions in the Finger Area in northern Sikkim in the past few years are aimed at opening a fresh front against India. Beijing has decided to put the historically undisputed border with Sikkim back into contestation. Concerns are growing about covert Chinese intrusions into the Indian territory to strengthen its claims on the disputed border areas. Chinese forces are regularly intruding into Bhutanese territory at the tri-junction with India and destroying Indian Army posts.[43] These incursions are strategically aimed as they are precariously close to India's "chicken-neck" — the Siliguri corridor which links the northeast passage. Chinese intrusions into the nondelineated parts of Bhutan's northern border with Tibet are also aimed at forcing Bhutan to settle its boundary issue with China. In April 2013, a Chinese military patrol set up camps several kilometers within the Indian side of the Line of Actual Control. This was the first time since 1986 that Chinese troops have refused to vacate their positions after being discovered.

After it emerged that the Chinese patrol had pitched camp in the Despang area of Ladakh, Indian media reported that two Chinese helicopters violated Indian airspace in an attempt to provide air cover to the soldiers. New Delhi summoned the Chinese ambassador immediately and sent military reinforcements to the region. It took China 3 weeks to order the military to go back.

China's rapid expansion and modernization of its transport infrastructure across the border is forcing India to respond though India is already decades behind. The build-up of infrastructure in Tibet should have rung alarm bells in Delhi long back, but no response was forthcoming. China's transportation modernization plans across the Himalayas had been evident for decades. Yet India chose to be lackadaisical in its approach without demonstrating a sense of urgency that this critical national security requirement demanded. Improved infrastructure helped China to rapidly deploy troops in Tibet when riots broke out there in 2008. The railway link between Beijing and Lhasa further tightens China's grip on Tibet. China's ambition is to extend the Beijing-Lhasa rail line to Yatung just a few miles from Sikkim's Nathu La and subsequently extend this to Nyingchi, north of Arunachal Pradesh, at the tri-junction with Myanmar. China's ambitions about the development of its border areas contrast vividly with India's tentative stance on infrastructure development.

China's transformation of the transport infrastructure in Yunnan, Tibet, and Xinjiang, the provinces that border South Asia, and its decision to build road and rail networks across the borders of these areas has transformed geopolitics in India's vicinity. India is struggling to cope with the decay in its border infrastructure.[44] It has only recently started building several tactically important roads along the China border in the eastern and western sectors. A number of airstrips are being upgraded so as to give India the ability to deploy a large number of troops in forward areas on short notice. Myanmar has agreed to allow China to use its land to build a highway to connect Kunming in its southeast with Chittagong in Bangladesh. Once built, the highway will allow China direct access to the Bay of Bengal, and it will run very close to the northeastern Indian states of Tripura and Mizoram. China has set up an in-house training facility for Su-30 fighter aircraft pilots of the Indonesian Air Force at the Hasanuddin Air Base where the unit is based. As a result, Chinese pilots will be flying much closer to India's Andaman Nicobar Islands.

The penetration of China into the Indian intelligence apparatus is growing to the consternation of many. India's premier National Informatics Centre, which governs and hosts all government websites as well as computers of the Prime Minister's Office, the Ministry of External Affairs, several Indian embassies, the Bhabha Atomic Research Centre, and the Dalai Lama were infected by GhostNet, a China-based cyber espionage network.[45] Though this came to light in early 2009, it has been going on for the last several years. China has been giving cyber warfare serious thought and has incorporated it into its military planning and strategy by encouraging civilian computer hackers to penetrate the computer networks of key political and military leaders in countries ranging from the United States to Japan, Taiwan, India and South Korea.

India Balances a Rising China.

China's recent hardening toward India might well be a function of its own internal vulnerabilities, but that is hardly a consolation to Indian policymakers who have to respond to a public that increasingly wants the country to assert itself in the region and beyond. New Delhi has responded to the challenge posed by a rising China by adopting a more hard-nosed policy vis-à-vis Beijing.

While there has always been and continues to be a range of opinions in India on how best to deal with China, a consensus seems to be evolving among the highest echelons of military planners and policymakers.[46] For a long time now, Indian defense officials have been warning their government in rather blunt terms about the growing disparity between the two Asian powers. The naval chief had warned that India neither has "the capability nor the intention to match China force for force" in military terms, while the former air chief had suggested that China poses more of a threat to India than does Pakistan. But the political leadership in India continued to act on the assumption that Beijing is not a short-term threat to India but rather needs to be watched over the long term. However, that assessment seems to be undergoing a change. After trying to ignore significant differences with China, Indian decisionmakers finally are acknowledging that the relationship between the countries is becoming increasingly contentious. Prime Minister Singh has suggested that "China would like to have a foothold in South Asia and we have to reflect on this reality. . . . It's important to be prepared."[47] The Indian defense minister has argued that China's increasing assertiveness is a "serious threat."[48] A former national security advisor and special envoy to China, M. K. Narayanan, has openly accused Chinese hackers of attacking his website, as well as those of other government departments.[49]

An elite consensus is evolving in India that China's rise is posing problems for the country. "We are friends, not rivals," said the Chinese Premier in India in 2010.[50] But a growing number of Indians now see China as a competitor, if not a rival. A 2010 Pew poll suggested that only 34 percent of Indians held a favorable view of China, with four in 10 viewing their neighbor as a "very serious threat."[51] More damaging is the perception gaining ground in India that China is the only major power that does not accept India as a rising global player that must be accommodated. The discord between the two countries thus remains entrenched, and their increasing economic strength and geopolitical standing has only underlined their rapidly growing ambitions. Though it is not entirely clear if China has well-defined policy objectives vis-à-vis India, Beijing's means, both economic and military, to pursue its goals are greater than at any time in the recent past. In response, a process of military consolidation and build-up of key external partnerships is underway in India.

Between 2010 and 2016, India is expected to spend $112 billion on capital defense acquisitions in what is being described as "one of the largest procurement cycles in the world."[52] The Indian Army is raising two new specialized infantry mountain divisions (35,000 soldiers) and an artillery brigade for Arunachal Pradesh aimed at redressing the imbalance on the Sino-Indian border. It is also revising its conventional warfighting doctrine that is aimed at deterring as opposed to dissuading China though its meaning in operational terms remains far from clear. The Indian military is currently refining a "two-front war" doctrine to fend off Pakistan and China simultaneously. Both fronts—the northeastern one with China and northwestern one with Pakistan—are being given equal attention. If attacked by Pakistan and China, India will use its new integrated battle groups to deal quick decisive blows against both simultaneously.

The Indian Navy is aiming for a total fleet of 140-145 vessels over the next decade, built around two carrier battle groups: the *Admiral Gorshkov,* handed over to India in November 2013, and the indigenous carrier, the 37,500-ton STOBAR Air Defense Ship likely to be completed by 2015. India's ambition to equip its navy with two or more aircraft carriers over the next decade as well as its decision to launch its first indigenous nuclear submarine are seen as crucial for power projection and to achieve a semblance of strategic autonomy. India's emerging capability to put a carrier task force as far as the South China Sea and the Persian Gulf has given a boost to the Indian Navy's blue-water aspirations and India hopes to add a third aircraft carrier by 2017, ensuring that the Indian Navy has two operational carriers at any given time.[53] The deployment of the *Jin* class submarine at Hainan by China will also force India to speed up its indigenous nuclear submarine project that has been in the making for more than a decade now with the Indian Navy, rather ambitiously, aiming at the induction of five indigenous advanced technology vehicle (ATV) nuclear submarines. A submarine-based nuclear arsenal is considered critical by Indian strategists to retain a second-strike capability.

The Indian Navy took command in January 2012 from Russia of the nation's first nuclear-powered submarine since India's last such vessel was decommissioned in 1991. With the induction into the Indian Navy of the Russian *Akula-II* class submarine K-152 *Nerpa*—now known as INS *Chakra*—India becomes the world's sixth nation to operate a nuclear powered submarine.[54]

INS *Chakra* does not really add to India's nuclear muscle as it will not be armed with long-range nuclear missiles. For that, the Indian Navy is still waiting for INS *Arihant*, an indigenous nuclear submarine, which is undergoing sea trials and is slated to become fully operational in 2014.[55] INS *Arihant* was formally launched by the Indian Prime Minister in 2009. This highly secretive project took more than a decade to complete and will fill out India's nuclear triad, with the submarine's ballistic missiles giving India a second strike capability.

What INS *Chakra* will do is to restore some muscle to India's underwater combat capability, which has been steadily depleting with only 14 conventional submarines holding forth. The Indian Navy has also lost critical expertise in maintaining and operating nuclear submarines, and INS *Chakra* is expected to be used for training sailors as well. India had leased a Russian *Charlie*-class nuclear submarine from the former Soviet Union in 1988 for 3 years. Indian naval planners are looking at nuclear attack submarines as an important element of their "denial strategy" (aiming to deny opponents' ability to use the sea, but without seeking to control it themselves), and as a response to any adversary's "sea control" strategy. Not only does a nuclear submarine enhance India's credibility as a major global military power, it is also seen as crucial in cementing the Indian Navy's blue-water status.

India is using its naval forces to advance its diplomatic initiatives overseas and in particular towards shaping the strategic environment in and around the Indian Ocean. Indian interests converge with those of the United States in the Indian Ocean region, and it is trying to use the present upswing in U.S.-India ties to create a more favorable strategic environment for itself in the region despite its historic sensitivities to the presence of U.S. forces in the Indian Ocean.[56] The United States has also recognized the importance of India's role in the region as was evident in Secretary of State Colin Powell's 2001 contention that it was important for the United States to support India's role in maintaining peace and stability in the Indian Ocean and its vast periphery.[57] More recently, in its first maritime service strategy update in 25 years, the United States views its sea power as the primary instrument in the U.S. defense arsenal to deter conflict with China, and cooperation with other countries' naval services, including India's, is recognized as crucial to fulfilling the strategic imperatives in the region.[58] The U.S. and Indian navies have stepped up their joint exercises, and the United States has sold India the USS *Trenton* (renamed INS *Jalashwa*), the first of its class to be inducted into the Indian Navy and marking a milestone in the U.S.-India bilateral ties. The United States would like India to join its Container Security Initiative (CSI) and Proliferation Security Initiative (PSI) but India remains reluctant. PSI is viewed as a U.S.-led initiative outside the UN mandate while the CSI would result in the presence of U.S. inspectors in Indian ports, making it politically radioactive. However, India has indicated that it would be willing to join the U.S.-proposed 1,000-ship navy effort to combat illegal activities on the high seas, given the informal nature of the arrangement.[59] India is seen as a balancer in the Asia-Pacific where the U.S. influence has waned relatively, even as China's has risen. India's ties with Japan have also assumed a new dynamic with some even mooting a concert of democracies proposal involving the democratic states of the Asia-Pacific working towards their common goals of a stable Asia-Pacific region.[60] While such a proposal has little chance of evolving into anything concrete in the near term, especially given China's sensitivities, India's decision to develop natural gas with Japan in the Andaman Sea, and recent military exercises involving the United States, Japan, India, and Australia, do give a sense of India's emerging priorities.[61]

India's decision to establish its Far Eastern Command in the Andaman and Nicobar Islands in the Bay of Bengal is aimed at countering China's growing presence in the region by complicating China's access to the region through the Strait of Malacca, the main bottleneck of oil transit to China. India has launched Project Seabird, consisting of the establishment of its third operational naval base in Karwar on the nation's western seaboard, an air force station, a naval armament depot, and missile silos — all at securing the nation's maritime routes in the Arabian Sea.[62] India is set to establish a monitoring station in Madagascar, its first in another country, as it is deemed vital to guard against the terrorist threat emanating from East Africa as well as to keep an eye on China's plan in the region. India also has its eyes on Mauritius for developing a monitoring facility at an atoll and has strengthened its naval contacts with Mozambique and Seychelles. India responded to Chinese President Hu Jintao's offer of military assistance to Seychelles by donating one of its patrol aircraft to the Seychelles Navy. India's support in the building of Chahbahar port in Iran as well as the road connecting it to Afghanistan is an answer to the Chinese-funded Gwadar port in Pakistan. India's air base in Kazakhstan and its space monitoring post in Mongolia are also geared primarily towards China.

India's "Look East" policy, originally aimed at strengthening economic ties with its Southeast Asian neighbors, has now led to naval exercises with Singapore, Thailand, and Indonesia. The Association of Southeast Asian Nations (ASEAN) member states have joined the Indian Navy in policing the Indian Ocean region to check piracy, trafficking, and other threats to sea lanes. Indian engagement of East Asia in the post-Cold War era has assumed significant proportions and remains a top foreign policy priority for the Indian leadership. The government of P. V. Narasimha Rao launched its Look East policy in the early-1990s explicitly to initiate Delhi's re-engagement with East Asia. Over the years, India has come to have extensive economic and trade linkages with various countries in the region even as there has also been a gradual strengthening of security ties. Present Indian Prime Minister Manmohan Singh has made it clear that his government's foreign-policy priority will continue to be East and Southeast Asia, which are poised for sustained growth in the 21st century.

India, too, has an interest in protecting the sea lanes of communication that cross the South China Sea to Northeast Asia and the United States. As India's profile rises in East and Southeast Asia, it is asserting its legitimate interests in the East Asian waters. As China expands its presence in South Asia and the Indian Ocean region, India is staking its own claims in East Asia. Most significant in this regard is India's growing engagement with Vietnam. India has decided to work with Vietnam to establish a regular Indian presence in the region as part of a larger Delhi-Hanoi security partnership, with Vietnam giving India the right to use its port of Nha Trang. Delhi and Hanoi have significant stakes in ensuring security of sea lanes and preventing sea piracy, while they also share concerns about Chinese access to the Indian Ocean and South China Sea. Indian strategic interests demand that Vietnam emerge as a major regional player and India is well placed to help Hanoi achieve that objective. It has been argued in Indian strategic circles that just as China has used states in India's periphery to contain India, Delhi should build states like Vietnam as strategic pressure points to counter China.[63] A common approach on the emerging balance of power is developing with India and Vietnam both keen on reorienting their ties with the United States as their concerns about China rise.

India has also accelerated its naval engagement with a number of Persian Gulf states, making port calls and conducting exercises with the navies of Kuwait, Oman, Bahrain, Saudi Arabia, Qatar, and United Arab Emirates as well as engaging with the navies of other major powers in the region such as the United States, the United Kingdom (UK), and France. It has also been suggested that to more effectively counter Chinese presence in the Indian Ocean and to protect its trade routes, India will have to seek access to the Vietnamese, Taiwanese, and Japanese ports for the forward deployment of its naval assets.[64] India is already emerging as an exclusive defense service provider for smaller states with growing economies that seek to strengthen their military capabilities in Southeast Asia and West Asia, such as Vietnam, Indonesia, Malaysia, Singapore, Qatar, and Oman, providing it access to ports along the Arabian coast, Indian Ocean, and South China Sea.[65]

India has moved to build strategic partnerships with many states that share its apprehensions about China: the United States, Russia, Japan, Vietnam, Indonesia, and South Korea. India's Look East policy that started primarily as an attempt to try and integrate India's newly liberalizing economy with that of the Asian tigers has now evolved into a more robust military-to-military partnership with important states in the region. India is providing support to Vietnam to enhance and upgrade the capabilities of its three services in general, and its Navy in particular. India is training Malaysia's Su-30 pilots and the Singaporean Army practices on Indian soil using cantonments and firing ranges. Indian warships now regularly visit countries across the region from Australia to Singapore and Indonesia.

While economic ties between India and South Korea have been diversifying across various sectors, defense cooperation between the two states has also gathered momentum, reflecting the rapid changes in the Asia-Pacific region's balance of power caused by China's rise. In 2005, India and South Korea signed a Memorandum of Understanding (MoU) on Cooperation in Defense, Industry, and Logistics, which was followed in 2006 by another MoU on cooperation between the two countries' coast guards. South Korea is one of the world's leaders in naval ship-building technology, and India would like to tap into South Korean naval capabilities to augment its own. As a result, naval cooperation is rapidly emerging as a central feature of bilateral defense working together with the two navies cooperating in anti-piracy operations in the Indian Ocean region and the Gulf of Aden.[66] Both states also share a strong interest in protecting the sea lanes of communication in the Indian Ocean region.

India is expanding its defense ties with Japan. Both Japan and India rely on the security of the sea lanes of communication for their energy security and economic growth. They have a shared interest in guaranteeing the free transit of energy and trade between the Suez Canal and the Western Pacific. With this in mind, they are developing maritime capabilities to cooperate with each other and other regional powers. The navies of the two are now exercising regularly, and the interactions between the coast guards is increasing with a view towards combatting piracy and terrorism, and cooperating on disaster relief operations.[67] Japan feels that only the Indian Navy in the region can be trusted to secure the sea lanes in the Indian Ocean, vital for Japan's energy security. It is also important for India to join hands with the much larger Japanese Navy, Asia's most powerful, to make sure that no adversarial power controls the regional waterways.

With a new robustness in its dealings with Beijing, New Delhi is signaling that there are limits to what is negotiable in Sino-Indian ties. In particular, it has adopted a harder line on Tibet by making it clear to Beijing that it expects China to reciprocate on Jammu and Kashmir, just as India has respected Chinese sensitivities on Tibet and Taiwan. Overriding Chinese objections, for example, the Indian government went ahead and allowed one of its central universities, the Indira Gandhi National Open University, to confer an honorary doctorate on the Dalai Lama.[68] This is the same government that just a few years back sent a note to all its ministers advising them against attending a function organized by the Gandhi Peace Foundation to honor the Dalai Lama so as to not to offend China.[69]

Ignoring pressures from Beijing, India also decided to take part in the Nobel Peace Prize ceremony for Chinese dissident Liu Xiaobo in Oslo, Norway, in November 2010. Beijing asked several countries, including India, to boycott the ceremony or face its displeasure, describing the prize as open support for criminal activities in China. India was among the 44 states that decided to participate, even as states such as Pakistan, Russia, Saudi Arabia, Iran, and Iraq were among the nations that did not attend. There were suggestions that the Chinese Premier might cancel his India trip in response, but nothing of the kind happened. Likewise, after Beijing began issuing stapled visas to the residents of Jammu and Kashmir and then denied a visa to the head of the Indian Army's Northern Command, New Delhi reacted forcefully and hinted that it was ready to review its long-standing Tibet and Taiwan policies. India also declined to endorse the "one China" policy during Wen's visit to India, a departure from past statements.[70] These developments are further evidence that India is reassessing its policy toward China as the latter's faster-than-expected rise has challenged the fundamentals of New Delhi's traditional approach to Beijing. India's robust partnership with the United States, its burgeoning ties with East and Southeast Asian nations as part of its Look East policy and its military modernization are all aimed at managing China's dramatic rise.

Indian policy trajectory toward China is evolving as India starts to pursue a policy of internal and external balancing more forcefully in an attempt to protect its core interests. The government is trying to fashion an effective response to the rise of China at a time of great regional and global turbulence. Though it is not entirely clear if there is a larger strategic framework shaping India's China policy, India's approach toward China is indeed undergoing a transformation, the full consequences of which will only be visible a few years down the line.

THE U.S. ROLE IN THE SINO-INDIAN MATRIX

With Sino-Indian friction growing and the potential for conflict remaining high, the challenge to India is formidable. India is increasingly bracketed with China as a rising or emerging power — or even a global superpower — though it has yet to achieve the economic and political profile that China enjoys regionally and globally. India's main security concern today is not the increasingly decrepit state of Pakistan but rather an ever more assertive China, whose ambitions are likely to reshape the contours of the regional and global balances of power with deleterious consequences for Indian interests.

India's ties with China are thus gradually becoming competitive, with a sentiment gaining ground among Indian policy elites that China is not sensitive to India's core security interests and does not acknowledge its status as a global player. India is rather belatedly gearing up to respond to China's rise with a mix of internal consolidation and external partnerships. The most important element in this matrix is India's emerging strategic partnership with the United States. New Delhi has looked to Washington for support as both Sino-Indian and Sino-U.S. competition has come into sharper relief in recent years. As Sino-Indian ties pass through a phase of turmoil, Washington will have to play the critical role of a balancer with even greater finesse than before. The United States has a key stake in the trajectory of Sino-Indian ties in view of the changing balance of power in Asia and China's growing assertiveness. As a new balance of power takes shape, India will be an indispensable element in that architecture, even as the United States remains a key player in managing the Sino-Indian dynamic. New Delhi will not be part of an explicit alliance framework with the United States against China but instead will look to the United States to manage the power transition in Asia and its attendant consequences.

The dichotomy between China and India's global convergence and their growing bilateral divergence has allowed India to collude with China as a power bloc against Western positions at the global level, even as at the bilateral level New Delhi is not averse to leveraging its relationship with Washington in order to constrain China. India's burgeoning relationship with the United States gives New Delhi some crucial strategic room to maneuver. China's rapid global ascent will bring the United States and India even closer, but India's traditional desire to retain strategic autonomy will preclude the emergence of any formal structure defining this bilateral relationship. India is beginning to receive attention from Washington as a rising power on a par with China. This process should continue with U.S. policymakers viewing Asia as a single region whose future will to a large extent be shaped by the trajectory of Sino-Indian ties. America's defense ties with India should be mature enough to deal with a range of problems in the Indo-Pacific. For this, the defense establishments in both states need to be aware of each other's requirements. That process has only just begun and needs greater political direction.

The United States faces the prospect of an emerging power transition in Asia, and a robust partnership with India will go a long way towards stabilizing the strategic landscape in the region. This is especially true at a time when China's faster-than-expected rise is generating widespread apprehensions. The United States should encourage New Delhi to enhance its presence further in East and Southeast Asia. That process is already underway, but India needs to do a better job of articulating its readiness to emerge as a credible actor in the region. The United States can help by encouraging its allies and partners in the region to engage with India more substantively.

Although it is clearly in the interest of both China and India to stabilize their relationship by seeking out convergent issue areas, a troubled history, coupled with the structural uncertainties engendered by their simultaneous rise, is propelling the two Asian giants on a trajectory that they might find rather difficult to navigate in the coming years. Pursuing mutually desirable interests does not inevitably produce satisfactory solutions to strategic problems. Sino-Indian ties have entered turbulent times, and they are likely to remain there for the foreseeable future.

ENDNOTES

1. M. Krasna, "Three Main Stages in the Development of Sino-Indian Contacts During the Indian Freedom Movement," *Archiv Orientalni*, Vol. 49, No. 3, 1981.

2. India-China, *Agreement between the Republic of India and the People's Republic of China on Trade and Intercourse Between Tibet Region of China and India*, April 29, 1954, available from *www.commonlii.org*.

3. For a detailed account, see S. Hoffmann, *India and the China Crisis*, Berkeley, CA: University of California Press, 1990. Also an earlier account by N. Maxwell, *India's China War*, London, UK: Jonathan Cape, 1970, is quite critical of Nehru and his "Forward Policy."

4. India-China, *Joint Press Communiqué*, December 23, 1988, available from *www.fmprc.gov.cn*.

5. "China is Threat No.1, Says Fernandes," *Hindustan Times*, May 3, 1998.

6. A. B. Vajpayee, "Letter [to William Clinton]," *The New York Times*, May 13, 1998.

7. A. Joseph, "When to Seek Resolution of Border Dispute," *Indian Express*, March 15, 2005.

8. India-China, *Declaration on Principles for Relations and Comprehensive Cooperation Between the People's Republic of China and the Republic of India*, June 23, 2003, available from *www.fmprc.gov.cn*.

9. A. Baruah, "China Keeps Its Word on Sikkim," *The Hindu*, May 7, 2004.

10. J. Dixit, "A New Security Framework," *The Telegraph* (Kolkatta), May 17, 2004.

11. M. Singh, "Address to the Nation," June 24, 2004, available from *meaindia.nic.in*.

12. India-China, *A Shared Vision for the 21st Century of the People's Republic of China and the Republic of India*, January 15, 2008, available from *www.fmprc.gov.cn*.

13. *Ibid*. It also had something of particular interest to India:

> The Indian side reiterates its aspirations for permanent membership of the UN Security Council. The Chinese side attaches great importance to India's position as a major developing country in international affairs. The Chinese side understands and supports India's aspirations to play a greater role in the United Nations, including in the Security Council.

14. "India-Russia-China Axis Hinted at After Kosovo Strikes," *The Associated Foreign Press*, March 28, 1999. Also see "Russia, China, India Pile up Pressure on West over Kosovo," *The Indian Express*, New Delhi, India, March 26, 1999.

15. James Clad, "Convergent Chinese and Indian Perspectives on the Global Order," Francine R. Frankel and Harry Harding, eds., *The India-China Relationship: What the United States Needs to Know*, New York: Columbia University Press, 2004, pp. 267–293.

16. *Ibid.*

17. Edward R. Fried and Philip H. Trezise, *Oil Security: Retrospect and Prospect*, Washington, DC: Brookings Institution Press, 1993, p. 1.

18. Siddhartha Varadarajan, "India, China Primed for Energy Cooperation," *The Hindu*, Chennai, January 13, 2006.

19. Pranab Dhal Samanta, "N-energy, UN: China and India Signal Friendship, Not Rivalry," *The Indian Express*, New Delhi, India, January 15, 2008.

20. Vandana Hari, "India and China: An Energy Team?" *Business Week*, December 6, 2005.

21. For a broad discussion about the Sino-Indian convergence on global issues, see Harsh V. Pant, *The China Syndrome: Grappling With an Uneasy Relationship*, New Delhi, India: HarperCollins, 2010, pp. 15-36.

22. "China Blocked India's ADB Plan over Arunachal, Confirms Krishna," *Indian Express*, July 10, 2009.

23. Yuriko Koike, "The Struggle for Mastery of the Pacific," *Project Syndicate*, May 12, 2010, available from *www.projectsyndicate.org/commentary/koike5/English*.

24. C. Raja Mohan, "A New Challenge," *Indian Express*, August 31, 2010.

25. Selig S. Harrison, "China's Direct Hold on Pakistan's Northern Borderlands," *International Herald Tribune*, August 26, 2010.

26. Pranab Dhal Samanta, "More than Troops, Chinese Projects in PoK Worry India," *Indian Express*, September 5, 2010.

27. On the problems confronting Indian defense policy, see Stephen Cohen and Sunil Dasgupta, *Arming without Aiming: India's Military Modernization*, Washington, DC: Brookings Institution, 2010.

28. SandeepUnnithan, "Indian Army not Ready for War with China," *India Today*, October 29, 2011.

29. Thomas Kane, *Chinese Grand Strategy and Maritime Power*, London, UK: Frank Cass, 2002, p. 139.

30. Youssef Bodansky, "The PRC Surge for the Strait of Malacca and Spratly Confronts India and the US," *Defense and Foreign Affairs Strategic Policy*, Washington, DC, September 30, 1995, pp. 6-13.

31. Manu Pubby, "China's New N-Submarine Base Sets Off Alarm Bells," *Indian Express*, May 3, 2008.

32. Bill Gertz, "China Builds Up Strategic Sea Lanes," *The Washington Times*, January 18, 2005.

33. For a detailed explication of the security ramifications of the Chinese "string of pearls" strategy, see Gurpreet Khurana, "China's 'String of Pearls' in the Indian Ocean and Its Security Implications," *Strategic Analysis*, Vol. 32, No. 1, January 2008, pp. 1-22.

34. For a nuanced analysis of this, see Andrew Selth, "Chinese Military Bases in Burma: The Explosion of a Myth," Regional Outlook Paper No. 10, Brisbane, Australia: Griffith Asia Institute, 2007.

35. Ziad Haider, "Oil Fuels Beijing's New Power Game," *Yale Global Online*, available from *yaleglobal.yale.edu/content/oil-fuels-beijings-new-power-game*.

36. Manu Pubby, "Indian Submarine, Chinese Warships Test Each Other in Pirate Waters," *Indian Express*, February 5, 2009.

37. Ben Bland and Girija Shivakumar, "China Confronts India Navy Vessel," *Financial Times*, August 31, 2011.

38. "China Against India, Pakistan Joining Nuclear Club," *Press Trust of India*, June 29, 2004.

39. Andrew Scobell, *China and Strategic Culture*, Carlisle, PA: Strategic Studies Institute, U.S. Army War College, 2002, p, 19, available from *www.strategicstudiesinstitute.army.mil/pubs/download.cfm?q=60*.

40. Mark Hibbs, "Pakistan Deal Signals China's Growing Nuclear Assertiveness," Nuclear Energy Brief, Washington, DC: Carnegie Endowment for International Peace, April 27, 2010, available from *www.carnegieendowment.org/2010/04/27/pakistan-deal-signals-china-s-growing-nuclear-assertiveness/4su*.

41. Dai Bing, "India and China's Great Game in Full Swing," *China.org.cn*, October 22, 2010.

42. Siddharth Srivastava, "India Hones Its Missile Shield," *Asia Times*, April 16, 2011.

43. Nirmalya Banerjee and Amalendu Kundu, "Chinese Troops Destroy Indian Posts, Bunker," *Times of India*, December 1, 2007.

44. See C. Raja Mohan, "Drawn In at the Borders," *South Asia Monitor*, September 18, 2010.

45. Dipanjan Roy Chaudhury, "China's E-Espionage," *India Today*, March 30, 2009.

46. For a good typology of India's China debate, see Mohan Malik, "Eyeing the Dragon: India's China Debate," Special Assessment, Honolulu, HI: Asia-Pacific Center for Security Studies, December 2003, available from *www.apcss.org/Publications/SAS/ChinaDebate/ChinaDebate_Malik.pdf*.

47. "PM Warns on China's South Asia Foothold," *Indian Express*, September 7, 2010.

48. Rajat Pandit, "Assertive China a Worry, says Antony," *Times of India*, September 14, 2010.

49. "Chinese Hacked PMO Computers, says Narayanan," *Indian Express*, January 19, 2010.

50. Jim Yardley, "In India, Chinese Leader Pushes Trade," *The New York Times*, December 16, 2010.

51. For details of this poll, see "Key Indicators Database: Opinion of China, Percent Responding Favorable, All Years Measured," Washington, DC: Pew Global Attitudes Project, available from *pewglobal.org/database/?indicator=24&survey=12&response=Favorable&mode=table*.

52. "Opportunities in the Indian Defence Sector: An Overview," KPMG, May 1, 2010, available from *www.kpmg.com/IN/en/IssuesAndInsights/ThoughtLeadership/Opportunities_in_the_Indian_Defence_Sector.pdf*.

53. Manu Pubby, "3rd Aircraft Carrier to be Inducted by 2017: Antony," *Indian Express*, May 17, 2007.

54. "INS Chakra Inducted into Navy," *The Hindu*, April 4, 2012.

55. K. V. Prasad, "INS Arihant on track," *The Hindu*, December 3, 2011.

56. On the recent trends in U.S.-India ties, see Harsh V. Pant, *Contemporary Debates in Indian Foreign and Security Policy: India Negotiates Its Rise in the International System*, New York: Palgrave Macmillan, 2008, pp. 19-38.

57. Colin Powell, "US Looks to Its Allies for Stability in Asia and the Pacific," *International Herald Tribune*, January 27, 2001.

58. "United States: New Naval Strategy," *International Herald Tribune*, October 25, 2007.

59. Sandeep Dikshit, "Join Global Policing of Sea Lanes, US Asks India," *The Hindu*, April 19, 2007.

60. On India-Japan maritime cooperation, see Gurpreet Khurana, "Security of Sea-Lanes: Prospects for India-Japan Cooperation," *Strategic Analysis*, Vol. 31, No. 1, January 2007, pp. 139-150.

61. On India's strategic priorities in the Asia-Pacific, see Harsh Pant, "India in the Asia-Pacific: Rising Ambitions with an Eye on China," *Asia-Pacific Review*, Vol. 14, No. 1, May 1, 2007 pp. 54-71.

62. Yevgeny Bendersky *et al.*, "India's Project Seabird and the Indian Ocean's Balance of Power," *Power and Interest News Report*, July 20, 2005.

63. Bharat Karnad, "Good Morning 'Nam'," *Asian Age*, July 7, 2011.

64. Mohan Malik, "Chinese Strategy of Containing India," *Power and Interest News Report*, February 6, 2006.

65. Pranab Dhal Samanta, "Start Getting Used to DSP: Defence Services Provider," *Indian Express*, January 1, 2008.

66. Siddharth Varadarajan, "As Trade Soars, India and Korea Push 'Strategic' Side to Ties," *The Hindu*, March 25, 2012.

67. Indrani Bagchi, "Japan, India Can Restore Peace, Stability in Asia-Pacific Region," *Times of India*, April 28, 2012.

68. Anubhuti Vishnoi, "MEA Gives Nod to IGNOU for Doctorate to Dalai Lama," *Indian Express*, April 24, 2011.

69. "Pleasing Beijing, Govt Tells its Ministers Don't Attend Dalai Lama Honour Function," *Indian Express*, November 4, 2007.

70. Pramit Pal Chaudhuri, "China's Flip-Flop on Kashmir," *Hindustan Times*, April 15, 2011.